Good Morning Hope
"A Life of Purpose"

By Heather Martin

Acknowledgments

Cover Design: Jacob Martin
Inside Design: Jacob Martin
Editing: Heather Martin

Table of Contents:

Before you embark on this 30-day journey to a life of purpose, I want to challenge you to partner with the Holy Spirit as you endeavor to remove lies and accept God's truth about who you are and what you can do.

Your life is marked with purpose and destiny to do great things. It's not about your age, education, or life experience; it's about who God has created you to be and what He wants you to do while you're here on this earth.

In the following pages, you will find out what the Word has to say about the situations you face and how to confront them in godly ways. As we learn to confront things the right way, we make room for miracles to flow in our life and, in turn, affect those around us. I pray that you are stirred to action as you read the following pages; I know I was when I wrote them for you.

In Christ,
Heather

Adaptable

Capable of fitting a particular situation or use.

"Don't grumble against one another, brothers and sisters, or you will be judged…" James 5:9

Do you believe in yourself? Do you believe that you are capable of moving mountains with your words? Do you trust yourself? These are really good questions to ask yourself as you're walking through seasons of transition and change. That's what life is, isn't it, always changing and transitioning into who God has created us to be?

God has put within each one of us the ability to adapt to our surroundings WITHOUT compromising our values. In fact, adapting is required if we're going to be truly successful! The struggle is many people believe adapting to transition and change inevitably causes them to compromise. This does not have to be true for you.

I want to share something with you that I have observed in my time of ministry with thousands of people from every possible background you could think of; it can be summed up in James 5:9, *"Do not grumble against one another."* I have seen countless individuals fall into the same trap. They grumble about others for being in! You name it. "I can't believe they're addicted to pain medicine." "I can't be-lieve they cheated on their husband." "I can't believe they…(fill in the blank)." That, my friends, is grum-bling, and you can't afford to do it lest you find your-self in the same boat. You become what you criticize or grumble about. What's the point of adapting and not grumbling? When we face change that requires adapting, we often grumble. The longer it takes to adapt, the easier it is to grumble against those we are called to love. The enemy loves when we grum-ble because he knows we are one choice away from becoming what we grumble about.

DECLARE: I adapt well to change because I trust God has my best in store. I will practice self-control and not grumble against those around me; I will love. I can and will do this because I was born to adapt to whatever comes my way. Thank you, Holy Spirit, for helping me!

Notes:

_____

_____

_____

_____

_____

_____

_____

_____

Adventurous

Disposed to seek adventure or to cope with the new and unknown.

"You will make known to me the paths of life; In Your Presence is fullness of joy; In Your right hand there are pleasures forever." Psalms 16:11

Everyone is a natural-born adventurer, even YOU! If you don't believe me, you're believing a lie. If you do believe me, congratulations on embracing your journey.

If you've lost your spirit of adventure due to hardships or heartache, I can tell you there is still hope to live this life to the fullest. More importantly, the Father wants you to know that He created you for a purpose that carries impact and is full of adventure; your life is not boring (some of you just said, "Yes, my life is boring").

Let's talk. There are so many responsibilities involved in living well. I'm not talking about having the latest and greatest clothes, house, car, etc... I'm talking about living a life of purpose in the midst of great responsibility. It is easy to get bogged down by the weight of great responsibility, but that is not God's best for us, for YOU. You say, "Heather, how do I keep a spirit of adventure while doing the responsible (hard stuff) well?" I say, "Stop trying to do it alone." Be consistent in trusting God to show you what your adventure will look like and remember; it won't look like anyone else's.

Psalms 16:11 says, *"You will make known to me the paths of life."* That is a good Father who loves His children well. He is not expecting us to figure it out independently; He wants us to trust that His promises are good and always on time. He IS an on-time God.

Being an adventurer means you must be OK with not knowing it all and trusting that He (God) does. Saying YES to being responsible with eyes wide open to what is right in front of you equals adventure!

DECLARE: I embrace adventure; I am adventurous. I have the best co-pilot helping me navigate my own unique journey. Life is good. Life is fun. I am thankful for another day to live a life of God's adventure for me.

Notes:

_____

_____

_____

_____

_____

_____

Affectionate

Feeling or showing affection or warm regard.

"A new command I give you: Love one another. As I have loved you, so you must love one another. By this, everyone will know that you are my disciples, if you love one another." John 13: 34-35

Each of us expresses affection towards others in our own unique way. That is a good thing. Are you familiar with the 'Five Love Languages,' by Gary Chapman? If not, check it out. The 'Five Love Languages' gist is how people need/receive affection. They are gift-giving, quality time, words of affirmation, acts of service, and physical touch. People need and give affection the way it feels most natural to them.

In any relationship, it's important for you to express what you need regarding affection, and it's your responsibility to find out what they need regarding affection. This will help your relationships thrive. After all, we were commanded to love.

What do you do if you are a person that thrives on 'words of affirmation' but your spouse/friend/grandmother thrives on 'quality time'? What happens when the way we receive affection differs from the way someone close to us receives affection? Simple solution, we ask the Holy Spirit to help us love others the way He loves us. Yes, it takes practice, it's work, and you will be challenged to grow, but it will be worth it. Nothing in life worth really having truly comes easy. It's the same with affection; it takes practice. You know what they say, It's the same with affection; it takes practice. You know what they say, "Practice makes perfect." Practice loving people well. Make your Father proud by partnering with the Holy Spirit in loving people - even when it's hard or out of your comfort zone. Remember, you're not doing it alone or in your own strength; you have the best helper ever!

DECLARE: I am affectionate and love people the way they need to be loved. I accept the challenge of loving people that seem hard to love because I know the Holy Spirit will help me. It will be said of me that I love people the way Christ loves me.

Notes:

_____

_____

_____

_____

_____

_____

_____

_____

_____

_____

Ambitious

Having the desire to be successful, powerful, or famous.

"Whatever you do, work at it with all your heart, as working for the Lord, not human masters." Colossians 3:23

I believe that each person desires to do or be something significant, and I believe it is for a reason. If God sent His only Son, Jesus, to die for YOU, you must be someone of great significance. Putting pride aside, let's talk about being ambitious. Being ambitious is not bad; however, I believe it can become bad when we let pride slip in. Have you ever heard the term 'slippery slope'? It's the struggle of life to balance wanting to be successful and not becoming prideful because you've done something great.

Let's establish that God did not send His Son to die for you so that you could be just anybody… Jesus died so you could be SOMEBODY. In order to be somebody, you have to be ambitious. You must want to do something great. Notice I said, 'something great,' NOT something 'big' - there is a big difference between being something great and being something big. You were created to be someone great! You must believe in order to do!

11

God has put inside of YOU the ability to do something great. Let's establish what 'great' is… 'great' is being your best you. Do you know what your best 'you' is? It's OK if you don't; God will show you. That's why you are reading this; you need to know you were created to be successful.

What is success? Success is doing life right and doing life well; however; comparison comes in to kill what you believe is good for you. 'Good for you' may be loving your spouse and children well. 'Good for you' might be running a multi-million dollar company. Both aspirations are good if they are truly YOU.

Friend, aspire to be great; aspire to be YOU. God will help you navigate the path you walk into eternity, which will be successful. Enjoy it.

DECLARE: I am ambitious, and I will be successful here on the earth. God will speak to me and show me the best way. Pride will not trap me.

Notes:

_____
_____
_____
_____
_____
_____

Amiable

Friendly, sociable, and congenial.

"Do to others as you would have them do to you."
Luke 6:31

First, YOU are awesome! People like you and need you. Will everyone 'click' with you? No. Will everyone understand you? No. Will you make everyone happy, NO? Welcome to life. Regardless of strife, fights, and everything in between, you must understand that you are still an incredible person who will bless many by – being you. I give you permission to STOP trying to please everyone and permission to LOVE everyone. Jesus commanded us to love, but we don't have to hang out with everyone. What if we spent more time loving those that needed us and stopped stressing about those who don't care? <u>The world needs healthy people that love well, and we need to lead that charge.</u>

If we followed Luke 6:31… *"Do to others as you would have them do to you,"* what would the Christian world look like (because we can't blame the secular world, they're lost)? If we love like Jesus, we should be a people bursting with HOPE. I change my world by loving people well. YOU, too, can change your world by doing the same!

Jesus led by example in EVERY way; He washed the feet of the person He knew would betray Him to death. He did it well and with genuine love. Do we struggle to love those that say something bad about us? Not anymore.

We choose to sync ourselves with the Holy Spirit; we crucify our flesh and rise above every attack of the enemy. We will be known as a people that are amiable no matter what! We will trust God in the midst of the storm and in the midst of the calm because He will always guide us into what is true and right. Bless God for His goodness.

DECLARE: I am a person that is friendly. People are drawn to me because of Christ in me. I will open my arms to those who need me and love them well. I am not alone, and I am thankful for that. Jesus, you help me. I will make my Father proud by being a person that is friendly and kind. I will be this person because it is truly who I am. Amen.

Notes:

_____

_____

_____

_____

_____

_____

Compassionate

Showing or having sympathy for another's suffering(s).

"Therefore, as God's chosen people, holy and dearly loved, clothe yourselves with compassion, kindness, humility, gentleness, and patience." Colossians 3:2

Clothe yourself with compassion. What would that look like? Is it possible to walk around clothed in compassion? Like your favorite jacket or shoes, could you wear compassion the same way? Sure, we can all wear compassion when we want to, but do we wear compassion when we need to? These are good questions to consider.

We are God's chosen people, holy and dearly loved. Understanding that we are chosen, holy, and loved makes wearing compassion much easier. When we are confused about being chosen, holy, and loved unconditionally, we will fail at wearing compassion. Do you know what I mean? Imagine, you find the perfect top, the perfect color, the perfect fit, it's flattering, it's on sale - all super important things when you find your favorite top - imagine this when you're wearing compassion. What does it look like? It looks like Jesus. It fits perfectly, no matter the situation. Compassion looks like loving people who are going through hell and need help but don't know what to do, OR they know what to do and won't do it... and you still love them; that is compassion.

Remember when they tried to stone a woman in the Bible for committing adultery (John 8: 1-11)? Jesus knew she was guilty and deserved to be stoned; it was lawful, yet, He responded with, "I do not condemn you, go and sin no more." <u>Amidst what was lawful, Jesus did what was better; He showed her compassion and the love of a Savior.</u> We are called to be that in this world. We must wear compassion and do what is better above what is justifiable because people need a Savior, and we lead them to Him by clothing ourselves in compassion.

DECLARE: I clothe myself daily in compassion. I will not judge a person or situation; I will lead them to a Savior by showing them compassion. People need compassion, and I will show them what it looks like by wearing compassion in my daily life with the help of the Holy Spirit.

Notes:

_____

_____

_____

_____

_____

_____

_____

Considerate

Showing concern for the rights and feelings of others.

"Do nothing out of selfish ambition or vain conceit. Rather, in humility, value others above yourselves." Philippians 2:3

We have all been raised differently. No two families are the same. Trying to copy what one family does in hopes of improving yours is a hopeless ploy in a game you can't win. That being said, how do you show real concern for the feelings of others when you've never walked in their shoes? <u>I have a little gold nugget for you: None of us has walked in anyone's shoes but our own.</u> There may be similarities in things we have experienced, but it is not the same as walking in a person's shoes.

We mean well when we try to encourage people in life, marriage, parenting, and relationships, but, at best, it is our opinion of how we would handle that situation. So, how do we maintain a posture of being considerate without controlling a person to do what we think they should do? First, we must understand that we cannot control anyone. We can love them, listen to them, and pray for them, but we can't control them. We get frustrated when we have a brilliant idea for handling their situation, and then we get mad when they don't take our advice. That, my friend, is not considerate it's control.

To be considerate, you need to be genuine. You need to see the person and the situation and seek to understand what it might be like to be in their shoes. You need to ask them what they need from you, understanding that sometimes you cannot meet their needs.

Don't try to solve their problem; sometimes, a listening ear is all that is needed. People know when others are genuine or fake. Understand that being considerate in any situation may be all that is needed.

DECLARE: Even when it's hard, I will be considerate. I will not make assumptions about people or how I would handle their situations; instead, I will seek to understand. I will be a good listener, I will be genuine. I will be patient and kind as I seek to understand situations and circumstances because the Holy Spirit will guide me every step of the way.

Notes:

_____
_____
_____
_____
_____
_____

Courageous

Able to face and deal with danger or fear.

"Be strong and courageous. Do not be afraid or terrified because of them, for the Lord your God goes with you; He will never leave you or forsake you."
Deuteronomy 31:6

Do not be afraid. Done. Close the book; I'm an expert. I wish. The reality is who we really are comes out when we're afraid. In the day and age that we live in, all we have to do is turn on the news to terrify our souls. If we don't see it on the news, we hear about it from a friend or someone in the grocery line. You name it; we are bombarded with opportunities to be gripped with fear - fear of what the future holds, fear of the unknown, fear of dying, and so on. Fear is the devil's playground, do me a favor and get off the swing! Jesus has an amusement park available to you with all your favorite rides (if you don't like rides, your favorite food).

Imagine the courage it took for Daniel to stand in the lion's den! Imagine the courage it took for Noah to build the ark! Imagine the courage it took for Peter to walk on the water! Courage conquers fear. Courage laughs at the unknown. Let's laugh at fear; let's laugh at the unknown. Why? Because God wrote your final chapter, and it's eternal.

You must know who to trust to be strong and courageous and run from fear. You have to know why you trust who you trust. Life is not about chance, luck, or fairytales but about living. Living life means making mistakes, making messes, and making memories you love. It takes courage to make a mess or mistake and continue moving forward. So many people wallow in their mistakes, they live in regret, and they wish for something different. The great news is we can have something different, learn from our mistakes, and clean up our messes. We have nobody to blame for the courage we refuse to obtain. Courage is available to all, but few take it. Fear is of the devil; courage is of God.

DECLARE: I am a person of courage. When people look at me, they wonder how I do what I do because of my tremendous courage. Christ in me is my source of strength and courage. I will no longer shrink back in fear; I will rise to face fear with courage and WIN.

Notes:

_____
_____
_____
_____
_____
_____
_____

Courteous

Characterized by courtesy and gracious good manners.

"But everything should be done in a fitting an orderly way." 1 Corinthians 14:40

I have always told my children that good manners go a long way in helping them succeed in life - even if people are rude, you still use your good manners. There are no exceptions to this rule as far as I am concerned. When my children fight with each other, they know I will say, "It's easier to get along than it is to fight." It's easier to use your good manners than it is to be rude. It takes practice, but eventually, that statement is true because it becomes who you are.

Everyone has manners, but they're not all good. Everyone is confronted with rude people at some time in their life - it's inevitable. <u>Choosing to be courteous in the midst of rude or unjust behavior is hard; it's a muscle you must build to succeed in this life.</u> There will always be people who deliberately push your buttons to get a rise out of you. How you respond is entirely up to you. We blame people for our bad behavior, but it's no one's fault but our own for how we behave or respond. Opportunities are constantly being presented to us to build this important muscle of being courteous in ALL things. A person with good manners is a person that is courteous.

1 Corinthians 14:40 says, *"Everything should be done in a fitting an orderly way."* In order for this to be true in our lives, we must be courteous in every situation. When we understand that it's not just something that happens, but it is a muscle we must build; it makes it easier to practice being courteous to rude people. When someone is rude to you, it's an opportunity for you to flex your 'courtesy' muscle. I am not, in any way, saying that you become a doormat for everyone to walk all over; I am saying be courteous in your response to how you communicate with people. It pleases God when we behave in a way that seeks to unite and not divide people.

DECLARE: I am dedicated to building my 'courtesy' muscle. I trust the Holy Spirit to help me be courteous to rude people. I can do this!

Notes:

_____
_____
_____
_____
_____
_____
_____
_____

Diligent

Characterized by care and perseverance in carrying out tasks.

"And let us not grow weary of doing good, for in due season we will reap a harvest if we do not give up."
Galatians 6:9

When we do something we love, our level of dedication is high; however, when challenges arise (because they will), it becomes easier to make excuses as to why things aren't getting done. Being diligent in any task means you won't stop until it's done. Diligence is not for the faint of heart; it requires consistency, dedication, and the ability to overcome difficulty. Sounds fun, right?

<u>If you look at any successful person, you will find that the core of their belief system is the willingness to be diligent until tasks are completed.</u> Successful people don't quit; they persevere. How do you persevere when what you are doing is really hard? You maintain a posture of diligent actions that move you in the right direction until your task is completed. You surround yourself with people that don't make excuses; they create solutions - and if they can't, they find someone who can!

You were born to do something significant. In order

to accomplish something of significance, you will have to be diligent in doing whatever it takes to get you to your goal. Galatians 6:9 says, *"Don't grow weary in doing good; you will reap a harvest if you don't give up."* The challenge is not giving up before you reap.

I always say, "Anything worth really having will be hard work - but it will always be worth it." If you're looking for easy, do nothing. Just as the earth rotates around the sun and never stops, we must diligently do what God has created us to do, remembering He sent the Holy Spirit to help us. He's a good Father who wants to see us succeed in life. Be diligent by being a person of action.

DECLARE: Even when it's hard, I will be diligent. I will be known as a person who gets things done and doesn't make excuses. I will rely on the Holy Spirit's help to show me the best way for me, and I will not compare myself to others.

Notes:

_____

_____

_____

_____

_____

_____

Empathetic

The ability to understand and share the feelings of another.

"Therefore, encourage one another and build one another up, just as you are doing." 1 Thessalonians 5:11

Life matters, and how we live it does too! Remember the cliche, "Walk a mile in someone else's shoe?" It's easy to say but hard to do! In our world, opinions are posted like stamps on letters going worldwide. Some make you feel good; most make you feel bad. Oftentimes, you don't even have to ask for one because it's freely given. Holding one's opinion to themselves is not easily done!

For too many years, I believed that if I had an opinion, you needed to hear it. There was no love behind my need for you to know my opinion. I still have a lot of growing to do, but I'm happy to say (with the help of the Holy Spirit and godly mentors) I am growing up and away from my old self. I am so thankful for God's patience toward me!

We are ALL challenged in 1 Thessalonians 5 to *"... build one another up..."* What would our world look like if we did this instead of offering our opinion where it was never asked? Our world would be changed for the better, and people would once again have hope for their future. To be empathetic is to love others beyond what you think and understand that God in YOU is all that anyone will ever need. <u>Empathy is loving others like Christ loves you and never settling for the scraps of comparison or judgment.</u> For too long, we have let the enemy trap us with the lie that having an opinion matters more than God's truth about His creation. Love wins EVERY TIME, and every time LOVE WINS.

DECLARE: I am partnering with the Holy Spirit because, without His help, I will fail to love people the way they deserve to be loved. I WILL choose love over my personal opinion and bring pleasure to my Father in Heaven. I win because I love well and am genuinely empathetic towards all people. Amen.

Notes:

_____

_____

_____

_____

_____

_____

_____

_____

_____

_____

Exuberant

Filled with or characterized by lively energy and excitement.

"Though you have not seen Him, you love Him; and even though you do not see Him now, you believe in Him and are filled with an inexpressible and glorious joy." 1 Peter 1:8

As believers, we should exude joy. When the world looks at us, they should see exuberant joy. I can already hear all the voices out there saying, "Walk a mile in my shoes, and then tell me to walk in exuberant joy." The reality is life was never meant to be easy, but we don't like to hear that; however, the longer I'm on this earth, the more I realize how true that statement is! So, how do we live a life of exuberant joy in the midst of hardship and difficulty? Great question! We rely FULLY upon the Holy Spirit to help us navigate this thing called life. There is no other way to fulfill 1 Peter 1:8 successfully.

As a wife, homeschooling mom, pastor, and every other hat we all inevitably wear, the challenge is real. The fight to keep our joy intact is real. It's not easy, but it IS possible. It's a choice that we choose to make every day. Somedays are definitely easier than others. On the harder days, it's important to cling to the truths in God's Word. Nehemiah 8:10 says, "...

the joy of the Lord is your strength." So many people just read the Word and don't apply it; we've got to train ourselves to read it and APPLY it to our own personal lives.

How do we read the Word, apply the Word, and live the Word so that we can live exuberant lifestyles here on earth? Simply put, <u>we reject every lie that contradicts the Word of God, and we pursue His truth and find victory to live exuberant lives full of God's joy.</u> In pursuing His truth, we find the strength to face each day. You've got this; you CAN do it. You can live an exuberant life no matter what comes your way because you have the Holy Spirit and the Word of God.

DECLARE: I choose to partner with the Holy Spirit to live an exuberant life here on earth. I choose joy in the midst of hardship, trusting that God knows best. I am thankful for the challenges that come, understanding they are opportunities to grow. Amen.

Notes:

_____

_____

_____

_____

_____

_____

_____

Frank

Open, honest, and direct in speech or writing, especially when dealing with unpalatable matters.

"Speaking the truth in love, we will grow to become in every respect the mature body of Him who is the head, that is, Christ." Ephesians 4:15

Being 'frank' is oftentimes misunderstood as being rude. So, how do we communicate in a frank way without being misunderstood? How do we communicate our hearts frankly without being viewed as a jerk? Is it possible to be frank without being rude at the same time? The answer is it takes practice to perfect being frank without being viewed as rude. The point is, it IS possible. Side note: there will ALWAYS be 'those' people that choose to be offended no matter what you say or do... In this situation, take the high road and walk away. Sometimes, you just have to walk away and trust God. So, you've heard it said, "Practice makes perfect," and it is true. We need to practice the art of being frank while also practicing walking in love - it has to be simultaneous.

The challenge for most people is they don't know how to be frank without being rude. We can ask ourselves these questions moving forward: Is what I'm getting ready to say being said with love? If not, don't say it until you can say it with love. Am I connected to the voice of the Holy Spirit and what He thinks about this situation? If not, pray and get God's wisdom before you communicate.

<u>Being frank is a great tool for communication when it is done the right way, it allows for direct dialogue without 'sugarcoating' what really needs to be said.</u> Trusting the Holy Spirit to help you grow in this is key to success. Many people remain frustrated by conversations that didn't turn out how they expected because they didn't have the courage to say what they needed. Don't let the enemy lie to you; you can say what needs to be said - in love!

DECLARE: With the help of the Holy Spirit; I am growing into an effective communicator. I will practice being frank with people, understanding it must be done in love. I can do this; I can communicate effectively! Amen.

Notes:

_____

_____

_____

_____

_____

_____

_____

_____

Generous

Showing a readiness to give more of something, such as money or time, than is strictly necessary or expected.

"You will be enriched in every way so that you can be generous on every occasion, and through us, your generosity will result in thanksgiving to God." 2 Corinthians 8:2

In a world full of self-centered people, it can be a challenge to embrace a generous lifestyle, and that's exactly what generosity is, a lifestyle. It IS something that can be taught, learned, and lived. The greatest thing about a generous lifestyle is it's never too late to start. A willing heart is all that is required to pursue a life of generosity. I truly believe it is in the heart of every person to be generous, but the enemy has come in and polluted what was once pure, and it's time we shine a light in the darkness and take our dominion back! Praise God; we can do it!

The first thing we need to do to become successful at living a life of generosity is to get rid of the thought, "What's in it for me." <u>A truly generous person does not care what they get from doing something for someone else; they simply enjoy being generous.</u> Oftentimes, seeing the other person happy is all a generous person needs.

The tricky part with generosity is when we do something for someone else, and they don't respond the way we expected, or they don't seem grateful. What do we do then? Do we stop being generous? According to 2 Corinthians 8:2, *we've been enriched in every way so we can be generous on every occasion.* So, someone else's response to my generosity does not determine how generous of a person I am. I've decided in my heart to live from a place of overflow, and because of that, I overflow with thanksgiving to God. Remember, no one can control how we choose to behave and think. We are responsible for how we steward what we have.

DECLARE: Father, thank you for teaching me how to be a truly generous person with no strings attached. Thank you that I do not base my generosity on people's responses or the lack thereof. I purpose in my heart to be a generous person. Amen.

Notes:

_____

_____

_____

_____

_____

_____

_____

_____

Gregarious

Fond of company; sociable.

"Share with the Lord's people who are in need. Practice hospitality." Romans 12:13

Enjoying the company of others is an essential part of living a life of purpose. We need people. Sure, there are those that live completely disconnected and (seemingly) content, but that doesn't mean it's right. Even the Lord said in Genesis chapter 2, verse 18, *"It is not good for man to be alone; I will make a helper suitable for him."* If our creator knew that it was not good for us to be alone, how much more should we recognize that we need companionship? People make life better.

It's important to understand that as we talk about being gregarious, we also understand it's OK not to 'click' with everyone. Romans chapter 12 verse 18 says, *"IF it is possible... live at peace with everyone,"* meaning - sometimes we won't get along with certain people! The challenge is understanding that we may not get along with certain people, BUT we can still successfully love them the way Christ loves us. Dwelling on the fact that we don't click with certain people is a waste of our precious time; instead, we focus on those we do get along with and develop those relationships into healthy, fruitful ones.

A gregarious person is a person that makes room for others in their life. It's a choice. Everyone has the ability to host others well, sure there are those that have a natural gift for hosting, while others have to work a little harder at it - that's just how it is! Don't let comparison rob you of inviting others into your life. Look at those God sends your way, and choose to see how they make your life better and cause you to grow. <u>People are a gift, and our lives will improve when we view them that way.</u> Make every effort to embrace those who come across your path and ask God how you can be a good friend.

DECLARE: I am a gregarious person. I connect well with those I come in contact with. I have the ability to love even difficult people well. I will not compare myself to other people; instead, I will have the courage to be myself no matter what. Amen

Notes:

_____

_____

_____

_____

_____

_____

_____

_____

_____

Impartial

Fair and just.

"For there is no partiality with God." Romans 2:11

There are naturally those we connect with better than others; however, if God does not show favoritism, we shouldn't either. The Father is the ultimate example of how we should live and love. <u>The life of Jesus reveals how we can live a balanced life, not one according to the world's standard but heaven's standard.</u> It has become increasingly easy to strive for the wrong things because of how easily accessible information has become. Oftentimes we don't even realize how imbalanced we've become until someone has the courage to tell us.

Being impartial requires inviting people into our lives to hold a mirror up and show us when we have drifted over into the realm of excluding others because we've grown too comfortable. What does that mean? It means we limit who we spend time with based on how people make us feel or whether they provide comfort and joy. Don't get me wrong; it's important to do life with like-minded people that encourage us! However, if people don't fit our chosen criteria, we often become partial about who we spend our time with. Believe me; I get it. It's easy to become a creature of habit; life gets busy, and convenience can rule us. But is that God's best for us? Should we only connect with those that think and act exactly like us?

To be impartial requires that I be present. I must be intentional about those that are around me and understand that there is always an opportunity to be a blessing when people are around. It requires discipline to unplug and be truly present above the noise of phones, computer's, etc., but the payoff is well worth the investment. Investing in people is always worth it. To be like Jesus means we must pursue an impartial life and be open to connecting with those around us.

DECLARE: I am present and intentional about connecting with people. I am not partial to people based on who they are; I am impartial and full of love toward all people. The Holy Spirit is my guide in loving people well. Amen.

Notes:

_____

_____

_____

_____

_____

_____

_____

_____

Intuitive

Based on what one feels to be true, even without conscious reasoning.

"I keep asking that the God of our Lord Jesus Christ, the glorious Father, may give you the Spirit of wisdom and revelation so that you may know Him better." Ephesians 1:17

I aspire to be like Christ every day; some days, I am hugely successful, while other days, I fail miserably. On the days that I fail miserably, I look to the one who knows me better than I know myself, and I ask for wisdom and revelation to grow past where I am. As I run this race to the finish line, I understand that the Holy Spirit's intuition in my life plays a key role in my success. Without the Holy Spirit, I would fail miserably; I have proof! Too often, I have tried things my way and invited the Holy Spirit to watch me (not lead me) and wonder why I fall on my face. I have never done anything successful apart from the help of the Holy Spirit. He's a genius, and I am His lifelong student.

To clarify, what do I mean when I say that I rely on the Holy Spirit's intuition in my life? It means I understand that the Holy Spirit is smarter than me and wants me to succeed. It means that the Holy Spirit is my helper; He leads and guides me in the ways of truth and godliness. When we rely on the help of the Holy Spirit, our intuition accelerates to a place that surpasses our understanding. We need heaven's wisdom and revelation because let's face it, some things in life just don't make sense! When faced with impossible situations and hardships, we must realize we will get the answers we need. Trust your intuition. Trust the Holy Spirit.

Don't doubt the power of intuition when coupled with the help of the Holy Spirit; it's powerful. You are powerful because you are free from the lies of the enemy. Reject every lie that says you don't know what to do in any given situation. Trust God's word and lean on the Holy Spirit. You are never alone; you are never forsaken… Praise God; He's beyond good.

DECLARE: My intuition coupled with the help of the Holy Spirit, WILL move mountains in my life. I am not defeated; I am victorious. I trust the Holy Spirit and lean on Him in times of need. Amen.

Notes:

_____

_____

_____

_____

_____

_____

Inventive

Having the ability to create or design new things or to think originally.

"But you are a chosen people, a royal priesthood, a holy nation, God's special possession, that you may declare the praises of him who called you out of darkness into his wonderful light." 1 Peter 2:9

I am not my own, I can be rebellious and think I am, but it's not true (1 Corinthians 6:20). I cost a great deal, I cost a life, and so did you. Man's frustration comes from the need to control oneself and situations, yet, that is not God's best for us. <u>God's best is a partnership between Him and us.</u> Allowing Him to lead us into the ways of life here on the earth is the best decision any person can make, and if done correctly, life-changing.

God doesn't make mistakes; He created each person on this planet with an inventive nature and creativity, as it were. We are all creative in one way or another, yet we struggle to discover how creative we truly are by getting wrapped up in our need for control. If we feel out of control or not in charge, we fight against insecurity, and it blurs the truth of who we really are - a creative genius! If I am God's special possession - according to 1 Peter 2:9, that makes what I DO special/inventive.

The fight is found in rejecting the enemy's lies and partnering with the Holy Spirit so we can be the inventive person we truly are! The more we grow up IN CHRIST, the greater our capacity to see our purpose here on Earth. Remember, it's all about God's Kingdom coming to earth through our gifting's. *Seek FIRST His Kingdom, and ALL these things shall be added to you* (Matthew 6:33).

You truly are a masterpiece; I pray the eyes of your understanding will be awakened to see this truth that you will pursue God with every fiber of your being and encounter His goodness in every area of your life!

DECLARE: I am an inventive person because of my Creator God. I will not compare myself to anyone else. I trust God's best WILL come to pass in my life for His glory and honor. I am a creative genius growing into all God created me to be. Amen.

Notes:

_____

_____

_____

_____

_____

_____

_____

Passionate

Showing strong feelings or a strong belief.

"Whatever you do, work at it with all your heart, as working for the Lord, not for human masters." Colossians 3:23

<u>In a world where hard work is undervalued by a mindset of entitlement, we have to fight for excellence when we're surrounded by mediocrity.</u> What does that mean? Millions of individuals were never taught how to work at something with all their hearts because they were struggling just to survive. Millions of people live life just to get by and get through another day. I would never presume to know what goes on in man's heart (I've been wrong too many times); however, the fruit of mediocrity is everywhere. Do we quit in the midst of what seems hopeless, or do we adopt the mindset of mediocrity because it's running rampant all around us? No, of course not! We rise up and confront mediocrity with PASSION. To be truly passionate about living life captures people's attention because it's uncommon.

In Colossians 3:23, we are challenged to do EVERY-THING as unto the Lord, not for man. Imagine, for a moment, that we took the smallest (seemingly unimportant) tasks and did them as if we were doing them for the Lord. Would it change the way we do things?

For most, I'm sure we would adjust how we do things. I know, for me, it changed the way I behave as a wife, mother, and pastor! When I shifted my thinking, my attitude changed. I wanted to change the way I did everything (and believe me, I am a work in progress) because I'm committed to living a PASSIONATE life for the glory of God. He deserves my best. Me living my best life, full of passion and victory, is one of the best compliments I can give Him. It's hard work to live a life of victory because we must resist the enemy's lies. We must choose to rise above mediocrity, understanding our goal is an eternity with a perfect Heavenly Father. Praise God!

DECLARE: I am a PASSIONATE person pursuing a life of victory for the glory of God. I resist mediocrity and pursue excellence. My days belong to the Lord, and He will help me every step of the way. Amen.

Notes:

_____

_____

_____

_____

_____

_____

_____

_____

_____

Persistent

Continuing firmly or obstinately in a course of action despite difficulty or opposition.

"Submit yourselves, then, to God. Resist the devil, and he will flee from you." James 4:7

I hate the devil; I hate how he torments people. *He prowls around like a roaring lion looking for someone to devour* (I Peter 5:8). For many, that is their reality; the devil is ready to devour them. To the one weary from the battle and ready to quit, all they can see is the enemy ready to pounce on and destroy them. It's a tangible fear for too many people. Knowing who we are IN CHRIST is absolutely necessary if we are going to defeat the lies of the enemy! We have to believe we have authority over the devil because WE DO! Jesus said in Matthew 28:20, *"...surely I am with you always, to the very end of the age."* If Jesus is with us - ALWAYS - how can we be defeated by the devil? We give the devil access to us by the words that come out of our mouths; we allow him to come and torment us because of what we've said and the things we've done... BUT... there is always hope for a child of God.

We MUST be PERSISTENT in pushing back the devil, resisting his attacks; only then will victory come. <u>In order for there to be victory, there has to be an attack</u>

of some kind, and we must recognize where it is coming from so we can dismantle it with our WORSHIP.

When I learned the power of persistent worship, it changed the way I fought against the attacks of the enemy. I have disciplined myself to get on my knees and worship through to breakthrough - because I know I am not alone, Jesus is interceding for me (Romans 8:34).

The Bible CLEARLY says, *"...resist the devil, and he will flee."* He hates when you worship God; soak in His presence, and the devil will FLEE. Be persistent. YOU ARE STRONGER THAN THE ATTACK! Remember that, write it down, and hang it on your fridge.

DECLARE: I am persistent in my worship. I resist the devil, and he has to go! I am never alone; Jesus is with me always. Amen.

Notes:

_____

_____

_____

_____

_____

_____

_____

_____

Philosophical

Relating or devoted to studying the fundamental nature of knowledge, reality, and existence.

"See to it that no one takes you captive through hollow and deceptive philosophy, which depends on human tradition and the elemental spiritual forces of this world rather than on Christ." Colossians 2:8

What are you devoted to studying? Are you easily provoked by the words of others? Can you defend what you believe with proof? These are good questions to ask as you grow in your relationship with Christ, remembering that we are lifelong students of Christ.

Many people can captivate others with their words because of how passionate they are in delivering their message, but does that make them right because they are convincing with their words? That is why it is important to know who we are and why we believe what we believe. Nothing matters if it contradicts the Word of God!

In today's culture, if we like something, feel something, or believe something, that's all that matters; however, when the day comes that we must give account for how we lived, it will matter what we chose to be truths in our lives. It's not what sounds good, it's what IS good that counts, and we discover what is good and true in God's Word. There have been many a time that I was been deceived because my depth of understanding of who Christ IS and what

His Word says was not deeply rooted within me. Thankfully, we have a helper, the Holy Spirit, that never gives up on us. Praise God! Through consistent and disciplined prayer and study time, I have grown in my knowledge of Christ and His promises. Knowing Christ better helps us not to be deceived so easily.

DECLARE: With the Help of the Holy Spirit, I can be made aware of the deceptive talk that contradicts the Word of God. I am growing in my knowledge of Christ and who I am IN CHRIST. I CAN do all things through Christ, who GIVES ME STRENGTH. Amen.

Notes:

_____
_____
_____
_____
_____
_____
_____
_____
_____

Practical

Concerned with the actual doing or use of something rather than with theory and ideas.

"Do not conform to the pattern of this world, but be transformed by the renewing of your mind. Then you will be able to test and approve what God's will is— His good, pleasing, and perfect will." Romans 12:2

Practical application of God's Word in our everyday lives is absolutely essential for accomplishing God's will for our lives. So many God-loving, well-meaning people go through life never really knowing what they were put on this earth to do, and they become frustrated with life. Sure, there are moments when we hit a groove, and life seems to be moving in a way that makes us feel happy and satisfied, but then life gets hard, and we stall in life. There are ups and downs, highs and lows, and everything in between - this is what we call LIFE. Life is not always fun, but there are always lessons to be learned, even when it's not fun.

The struggle is not conforming to the things of the world that are daily before our eyes. Daily renewing our mind with the Word of God is the only way to traverse life here on earth successfully. Romans 12:2 says that by renewing our mind, we can test and approve God's will for our life. The challenge is to consistently renew our minds. I tell my children that they will NEVER be done reading their Bibles; they start from the beginning when they finish. Reading your Bible is not an option if you are going to live a life knowing what God's will is for you. The great news is, His plan for you is: good, pleasing and perfect! Don't look to man when God is the true source.

I am daily learning how to practically apply God's Word to my everyday life, even when my day doesn't go as planned! The level of obedience and trust required to do this is a small price to pay to walk in His fullness. Only you can choose what kind of life you will live. Only you are responsible for what you allow by what you say.

DECLARE: I am learning how to practically apply God's Word to EVERY area of my life with the help of the Holy Spirit. I am choosing to link arms with God through His Word to find my best life here on earth. Amen.

Notes:

_____
_____
_____
_____
_____
_____

Rational

Based on or in accordance with reason or logic.

"Being fully persuaded that God had power to do what He had promised." Romans 4:21

In Joshua 21:45, we see that not one of the GOOD promises the Lord had spoken failed; all came to pass. What an incredible heavenly Father that honors His promises to them that believe and are called sons/daughters of God. We are a blessed people.

To be rational in a very irrational world requires some foresight of what God has done for His children; it also requires that we know our role in our relationship with Father God. <u>One of the MOST important keys to living a life of purpose is learning to be rational, in other words, we respond to situations, not react to situations.</u> Learning how to respond versus react requires an individual to be rational in any given situation, no matter what it is. It's like building muscle, it takes discipline and practice, but eventually, if we don't give up, we grow into rational people that can handle any situation that comes our way.

I've grown a lot in the area of being rational, however; when my kids are hurt by someone, I want to react and protect them. When my children lie, I want to react to their wrong behavior. It's an area for me to grow in. This is one simple example we can apply to many areas of our lives. I am thankful that we are God's workmanship, created IN CHRIST Jesus to do GOOD works (Ephesians 2:10). Let's not forget Romans 4:21, we MUST be fully persuaded that God has the power to do what He promised. If we believe God has the power to do what He's promised, it should help us grow into rational people that respond in love to EVERY situation. We CAN do it; we can be rational even when it involves our families, work, relationships, etc... Don't give up, and don't quit; you can do it!

DECLARE: I am growing into a rational person that can enter any situation with love, grace, and hope. I am submitted to the correction of the Holy Spirit as I learn and grow. I am not alone. Amen.

Notes:

_____
_____
_____
_____
_____
_____
_____
_____
_____
_____

Reliable

Consistently good in performance; able to be trusted.

Now it is required that those who have been given a trust must prove faithful. 1 Corinthians 4:2

I have a person in my life who can be trusted beyond all measure and is available to me no matter what may come - my husband. We don't always see eye to eye, but it doesn't affect how reliable Jacob is to me. Through thick and thin, highs and lows, good and bad, everyone needs someone they can rely upon! You need to be that for someone. I want to remind you of how important you are to others. What's inside you is a gift to someone else.

1 Corinthians 4:2 explains that WE must prove faithful. We must learn to do hard things well, like loving people in their mess for the sake of them repenting and being restored. I am NOT saying that we become a toilet for people to vomit into whenever they're having a bad day; I am saying that we learn to LOVE people in their mess because we have hope in Jesus. <u>People's messes' do not determine how much we choose to love them; it determines how much we need to pray for them.</u>

Growing into a reliable person requires self-control because we will be told things that must remain confidential. We have to be able to hear hard stuff because people are dealing with hard issues. When we are reliable to those around us, we demonstrate the heart of Jesus to them because Jesus is the most reliable person. Don't grow weary about people failing or forsaking you because we do everything for the Lord (Colossians 3:17).

Jesus is with you until the end of time (Matthew 28:20). It will always be about us becoming more like Jesus to everyone we encounter, but we can't do it without the help of the Holy Spirit. The good news is the Holy Spirit loves to help us; we just have to ask. Growing up can be hard, but the fruit of growing is worth the growing pains.

DECLARE: I commit to growing daily into a reliable person that sees the best in those around me. The Holy Spirit has permission to correct me when I get off track. I am reliable. Amen.

Notes:

_____

_____

_____

_____

_____

_____

_____

Resourceful

Having the ability to find quick and clever ways to overcome difficulties.

"If any of you lacks wisdom, you should ask God, who gives generously to all without finding fault, and it will be given to you." James 1:5

Who is to blame if we need help with something but don't ask for help? Too many times, our pride gets in the way of us asking for help. The devil tricks us into thinking more of ourselves than we should, so we don't reach out and ask for help because we don't want it to affect the way people view us. Pride is a dangerous, sneaky thing that slither's into our lives through wrong thoughts. People are great for showing us blind spots in our lives IF we are willing to listen to them.

A resourceful person knows that difficulties are a part of life, and having the right tools to overcome those difficulties is essential to one's victory. <u>The ability to overcome difficulty is made easier when we know the best resources available to us, the Bible and Holy Spirit.</u> James 1:5 says *to ask God for wisdom, and He will give it to you.* Meaning God has the wisdom I need to overcome difficulty, BUT I have to ask Him for it. In my short years on this earth, I have learned many valuable life lessons, one being that I have to open my mouth and ask God for specific help. It is my job to ask and believe God and His Word. We muck it up when we try to do it alone. We NEED a Savior to show us the best way, and He is not far from us (Acts 17:27). God is not our genie in a bottle that we call on to save us from hardship, He has equipped us with what is needed and made us resourceful human beings. Look at all the great inventors and creators in the world, God made them, and He made YOU too!

Every day, month, and year is a gift to grow into an amazing person that carries more authority and power everywhere you go. We will not be the same people next year that we are today. We are called to blaze a trail for God's glory here on the earth through the resources He has provided. What a brilliant Heavenly Father we serve!

DECLARE: I commit myself to the Lord in greater ways today; I choose to connect with Heaven's resources and grow. I will not let pride get in the way of my growing into a resourceful person. Amen.

Notes:

_____

_____

_____

_____

Sensible

Perceiving through the senses or mind.

"The prudent see danger and take refuge, but the simple keep going and pay the penalty." Proverbs 22:3

Have you ever found yourself talking to someone and thinking, "They have no common sense about life; how have they survived this long?" Has the stupidity of people ever dumbfounded you? If we're being transparent, we will ALL admit there have been times we talk to people and wonder how they're survived this long. I'm not being mean; I'm being honest. It's sad that many people didn't have parents to teach them common sense life skills. Most of these people are in survival mode, trying to make it through another day.

To assume that people should just be sensible about certain things is to overlook what made them the way they are today. Proverbs 22:3 says t*hat the prudent (smart people) see danger and hide while the simple (lacking common sense) keep going and suffer.* People in constant conflict and turmoil cannot be sensible, hence why they are always in conflict and turmoil. I am not talking about those that thrive on drama and conflict; I am addressing those that really need help because they were not taught true life skills.

We must lead by example when it comes to behaving sensibly because people are always watching. When our buttons are pushed, we behave sensibly. When we are tired, we behave sensibly. When we are mistreated, we behave sensibly. <u>We are not the proverbial frog that is being boiled slowly; we see trouble and jump out of the way!</u>

For me, raising four kids has been the hardest and greatest reward. They are always watching and always listening. It is a huge responsibility to steward myself and behave in a sensible manner in ALL things because it's not just about me; it's about those I influence. It is humbling.

DECLARE: I can do ALL things through Christ, who gives me STRENGTH. I am a sensible person that walks in grace toward others. I SEE trouble and run from it. I trust God in all things. He helps me. Amen.

Notes:

_____

_____

_____

_____

_____

_____

_____

_____

Sincere

Free from pretense or deceit; proceeding from genuine feelings.

"To be made new in the attitude of your minds; and to put on the new self, created to be like God in true righteousness and holiness." Ephesians 4: 23-24

People need sincerity and to know that the person they are talking to is genuine. I have been around insincere people, and it didn't feel good. Have you ever been around insincere people? How did it make you feel? When we get around condescending people that are insincere, it is an opportunity to evaluate what is going on in our hearts. No one likes to feel like less than who they are. So, when we feel less than awesome, we can ask the Holy Spirit to reveal what is happening in our hearts. Matthew 12:34 says, *"The mouth speaks what the heart is full of."* If our hearts are full of insecurity or lack of identity, what do you think will leak out? Yes, we leak out what is in our hearts on a daily basis, it's a great indicator of what we need to repent of or deal with.

That being said, do you find it hard to be sincere when you are around someone that is annoying to you? Side note: You can STILL walk in love and be annoyed by people. Real life is the best training ground for growing in our purpose. The challenge is learning to be sincere even with the most annoying person; it's a muscle we need to build! We have a lot of spiritual muscles we need to build, and that comes with consistent practice. Annoying people deserve to be treated sincerely with love, and you will fail if you try to do it with your own strength. Ask Holy Spirit to guide you into all truth and help you be genuinely sincere because it's the right thing to do in every situation.

I want you to remember that every test that comes our way is for our good, to help us grow into the image of Christ Jesus (Ephesians 4: 24).

DECLARE: I will be known as a sincere person. I will not be swayed by how someone acts; I will be swayed by the power of the Holy Spirit. I am committed to building big spiritual muscles for Jesus. Amen

Notes:

_____

_____

_____

_____

_____

_____

_____

_____

_____

Sympathetic

Feelings of pity and sorrow for someone else's misfortune.

"Be kind and compassionate to one another, forgiving each other, just as in Christ God forgave you."
Ephesians 4:32

Difficult things happen to ALL people. No matter how hard we try to avoid hardship, it comes knocking on our door. I don't say that to scare you; I say it because it's true; it's life. If you are alive and breathing, you know hardships. <u>Difficulty allows us to see Christ at work amid what feels like hell.</u>

With that understanding, let's look at the gift of being sympathetic to others walking through difficulty. People NEED sympathy, NOT pity when walking through difficult seasons. Sympathy says, "I am so sorry this is happening to you; let's pray." Pity says, "Here, let me try to fix this for you." The latter prolongs the inevitable because people have to face their own challenges to gain true victory. We cannot shrink back in hard times; we must run into the open arms of Christ and be led by HIM to victory. <u>Sympathy is coming alongside someone, offering them an ear to process what's going on, and challenging them to push through.</u>

The hardest thing about being sympathetic is knowing when it turns into enabling. You HAVE to be led by the Holy Spirit regarding loving people well. Well-meaning people get burned out by hurting people because they don't have an ongoing conversation with the Holy Spirit while walking through hardships with others. You ARE capable of being needed without being drained emotionally.

Be kind and compassionate to EVERYONE, forgiving each other, because Christ forgave YOU (Ephesians 4:32). We have been forgiven of much so that we can forgive others. We can sympathize with others and point them to Jesus; that is our goal.

DECLARE: With the help of the Holy Spirit; I can sympathize with others without enabling them to stay where they're at. I will assume the best about others and forgive quickly. Amen.

Notes:

_____
_____
_____
_____
_____
_____
_____
_____
_____
_____

Unassuming

Not pretentious or arrogant; modest.

"Reject every kind of evil." 1 Thessalonians 5:22

To walk humbly before God and man is a challenge in this fallen world, but it is absolutely possible! Why is it hard to maintain a spirit of humility? Lack of consistency. There is a fight for our souls; make no mistake. The devil hates you and wants to destroy you, but Christ came that YOU would have life and have it abundantly (John 10:10).

It seems like more people are fighting to prove who they are instead of trusting who they are. We live in a broken world that needs unassuming people to enter situations dripping with HOPE. We MUST be carriers of HOPE to insecure people fighting to discover who they are. The enemy wants us to assume the worst about people; God wants us to see GOLD. Sometimes people need help to discover the gold inside of them. Too often, our eyes are fixed on others instead of on Jesus, so we miss the gold He deposited in each of us.

Every kind of evil must be rejected by EVERY child of God no matter the cost because it's about our eternity. Temporary pleasures must not deter us from the race we are called to run. Our race is for the glory of God. Why do we insist on having our own way or voicing our opinion? People don't need that; they need unassuming individuals full of the love of Christ to enter their space and show them a better way because we know the best way — it is Jesus! What a gift we've been given to share the love of Christ by living our best life here on earth. <u>By living well and unassuming, we become a magnet for His glory and a net for those lost in an ocean of lies.</u> Jesus wants to use us to attract the lost to His Kingdom. He deserves our best, and the lost deserve it too!

DECLARE: I can do ALL things through Christ, who gives me strength. I choose to enter situations unassuming and full of HOPE. I will be a net to catch the lost from an eternity in Hell. I will go where He leads and say what He says. Amen.

Notes:

_____

_____

_____

_____

_____

_____

_____

_____

_____

_____

_____

Witty

Showing or characterized by quick and inventive verbal humor.

"A cheerful heart is good medicine, but a crushed spirit dries up the bones." Proverbs 17:22

Have you ever been around a quick-witted person who knows what to say? Sometimes a witty person is just what is needed to diffuse a messy situation. Sometimes, a quick bit of verbal humor can keep a conversation from blowing up in ones face! So many times, I have come down from an intense conversation by one funny comment, and nothing else mattered, and the issue resolved itself. It reminds me to get over myself. <u>We can get so caught up in justice and forsake mercy when we should embrace mercy and trust God!</u>

If a cheerful heart is good medicine (Proverbs 17:22), don't you think the enemy would like our prescription to run out - permanently? How do we keep our prescription FULL? We renew our minds with God's truths (Romans 12:2). The only way to combat the devil is to renew our minds and trust His Word is TRUE!

I do my best to surround myself with witty people because they make me laugh, and I like to laugh. Sometimes I watch funny videos if I need a good laugh. Joy is important to God; after all, He made it a fruit of the Spirit. Joy is not an afterthought; it's supposed to be a forethought. In other words, you CHOOSE JOY at the start of each new day. I have a sign in my house that says, "Today WILL BE awesome." I'm ever thankful for my constant companion in the Holy Spirit because He is JOY personified, and He lives in me!

Pray witty people into your life because prayer works. Wittiness is contagious, so surround yourself with more of it; you won't regret it! *Whatever you need, ask your Father, who is generous* (John 16:24).

DECLARE: I am a person that pursues JOY. I make the most of EVERY opportunity. Witty people are attracted to me and make me laugh. My life is full of laughter. Amen.

Notes:

_____

_____

_____

_____

_____

_____

_____

_____

_____

In closing on our 30-days of purpose:

You've just spent 30 days discovering what it takes to live a life of purpose. By simply adjusting the way you think about the life you live and the people you live it with, you are well equipped to defeat the lies of the enemy and live a life of
purpose every day of your life.

There will be challenges and setbacks, but trust in the Lord with ALL your heart and lean not on your own understanding. He will guide you into a life of purpose because that's how much He loves you!

Thank you for investing in yourself, and thank you for partnering with me as we do our part to see God's Kingdom manifested here on the earth through His children. The best is yet to come!

Until next time….

Love,
Heather

Made in the USA
Middletown, DE
03 August 2023

35835261R00036